How to Architect

How to Architect

Doug Patt

The MIT Press
Cambridge, Massachusetts
London, England

For information about special quantity discounts, please email special_sales@mitpress.mit.edu

This book was set in Adobe Garamond and Univers by the MIT Press Printed and bound in the United States of America.

Library of Congress Cataloging-in-Publication Data

Patt, Doug, 1968–

How to architect / Doug Patt.

   p. cm.

ISBN 978-0-262-51699-0 (pbk. : alk. paper) 1. Architecture. I. Title.

NA2550.P38 2012

720—dc23

2011024384
10 9 8 7 6 5

Thanks Morty

Contents

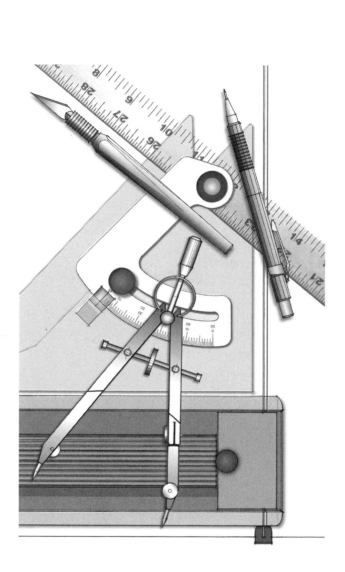

Preface

The word "architect" is a noun, but I like to use it as a verb. This misuse has kicked off some lively discussions about architecture and language, and the effect of using parts of speech and parts of buildings in different ways than were intended. Buildings are like sentences. They have a structure. They follow rules. But when you break the rules, it doesn't always mean that you've ruined the place, or the expression. Changing the function of a word, or room, can also produce surprise and meaning. Exceptions can produce inflections, and misuse can lead to invention.

This book is about how to architect. You can think of it as a starter book—a place to begin. It grew out of the videos I create and post on the Internet at YouTube and howtoarchitect.com. If you are thinking of going to school to become an architect, or considered it once but changed your mind—or if you simply have a street interest in buildings—this book won't hurt you. Take it for what it is: first letters, not final words. If you are a practicing architect, it may remind you of some of the things that drew you to the profession before you were licensed, and how much smarter you are now than then. If you are like me, you have probably asked yourself at one time or another: what is architecture? and what is an architect? This book addresses those questions in simple, A–Z terms.

I'm a big fan of hand drawing and lettering, so I introduce each entry with a hand-drawn letter. Beneath each letter is a brief discussion of the highlighted term in relation to the practice of architecture, or an attempt to show why the particular thing or idea I'm presenting might belong in the architect's lexicon. Like most architects, I prefer pictures to words, and I'm a lot more secure drawing than writing, so I make use of drawings to reinforce some points, and I include photographs and computer-generated images for the same reason.

I've found over the years that a big complaint from high school students and their parents is that guidance counselors are generally not equipped to discuss the profession of architecture with students, or to give much guidance to students who want to become architects. I also meet many people, well beyond their college years, who either worry about the fact that their children want to become architects or think that architecture is a dispensable profession. This book is meant to give encouragement to aspiring architects, but it also acknowledges that the opposite urge exists: the urge to deny the young their architectural wish. For as much as we are fascinated by architecture, our culture also has a tendency to suppress architectural fantasy and desire—to marginalize architecture and those who practice it as superfluous. Against those who would say *build, but do not use an architect*, this book is a defiant verb. Architect!

LINES
OVERLAP

DYNAMIC
ANGLE

90°

ASYMMETRY

A IS FOR ASYMMETRY

Asymmetry is the opposite of symmetry. A mirror provides a symmetrical reflection whereby the surface of the mirror is the axis through which space is divided. When an object is divided by an axis and the sides don't match, the object is asymmetrical. Our bodies appear symmetrical, but they are not. One foot may be larger than the other, one leg longer than the other, or an eye or eyebrow not quite the same shape as its opposite. An automobile appears symmetrical from the outside, but the interior is not. So too with our brains. While they appear symmetrical on the outside, the role of each hemisphere is different. We've all heard of people being left-brained (analytic) or right-brained (creative). Likewise with buildings. Chartres cathedral only appears symmetrical. The cathedral's towers fall symmetrically on the facade but are clearly different. However, asymmetry is more common in modern and contemporary architecture. Buildings by Gerrit Rietveld, Le Corbusier, and more recently Frank Gehry, Zaha Hadid, or Rem Koolhaas make little attempt to be symmetrical. Buildings don't have to be symmetrical to be functional or beautiful.

The opposite of asymmetry is symmetry. When a hand is held to the surface of a mirror, its corresponding or symmetrical image is produced—equal and opposite. Symmetry has been an integral part of design for

Two different towers on an otherwise symmetrical facade of the Gothic cathedral in Chartres, France.

thousands of years and a telltale sign that the building has a statement to make. The pyramids in Egypt, many soaring cathedrals of the world, the Taj Mahal, great classical works, the temples of Asia and ancient Rome and Greece, as well as many of the great cities of the world are clear examples of symmetry. We find symmetry in the work of some of the great modern and contemporary architects like Frank Lloyd Wright, Mies van der Rohe, Louis Kahn, Philip Johnson, Eero Saarinen, and more recently Santiago Calatrava.

Symmetry is an integral part of creating something beautiful. Interestingly, while many things in nature appear symmetrical, closer inspection reveals asymmetry (the human form is just one example). Perhaps this is why the ideal of symmetry remains such an important pursuit in the creation of beautiful objects. We want objects that we create to be similar to the symmetrical objects we seem to be. The architect uses both symmetry and asymmetry as tools for design, often blending them within a single work.

Top: Elevation of the Tempietto designed by Donato Bramante in Rome. This building is symmetrical. Bottom: Perspective of Notre Dame du Haut in Ronchamp, France. The architect Le Corbusier designed this very modern church. This building is asymmetrical. Look at the central vertical axis running through both buildings. Corresponding sides of the Tempietto are mirror images, while the corresponding sides of Notre Dame du Haut are not.

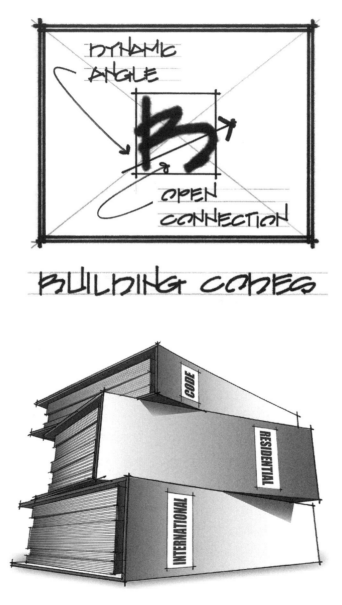

BUILDING CODES

B IS FOR BUILDING CODES

Bob Dylan sang that everyone "gotta serve somebody." That is, everyone has someone to answer to. Whether it's a boss on a factory floor or a board of directors, there are always rules to follow. Building codes, zoning ordinances, the Americans with Disabilities Act (ADA), and homeowners' association bylaws are rules for architects. Building codes set allowable standards of safety for buildings. They were created for the health, safety, and welfare of the public. Building codes differ across the United States and the world depending on local, state, and federal jurisdictions. Zoning ordinances dictate how a piece of property can be used, building size, accessory structures, and so on. These mandates vary widely in terms of geographic location and enforcement. ADA is a law that went into effect across the United States in 1990. For the architect, it provides rules about design and construction that ensure buildings accommodate the disabled. Finally, bylaws are rules created by local groups or associations (e.g., of homeowners). There is also a nonmandatory building standard for "green" building design called LEED (Leadership in Energy and Environmental Design). These rules were developed to affect a building's environmental, economic, and social impact.

It is the duty of both design and construction professionals to abide by mandatory parameters. Buildings are reviewed before and throughout the construction process for code, bylaw, and zoning compliance. Consequences for noncompliance vary but often mean the loss of time and money. Good architects follow the rules and use them to make better buildings. It may be surprising that even the most progressive, unusual, and creative buildings in the world were designed within building codes, zoning ordinances, ADA restrictions, and bylaws. Rules and regulations should never be looked at as prohibitive but rather as an opportunity. It is challenging to solve a problem in a creative and elegant way within constraints. Phil Knight, founder of Nike, said, "Play by the rules, but be ferocious."

Building codes have been around for thousands of years. Their roots can be found in documents like the Code of Hammurabi and the Hebrew Bible. Top: An excerpt from the 2006 International Residential Code. The IRC covers standards for many building elements such as fire protection, egress, construction materials, finishes, foundations, electrical work, etc. Bottom: A detail describing the elevation of a stair and handrail. The notes call out requirements from the IRC.

R311.5.3 Stair treads and risers

R311.5.3.1 Riser height. The maximum riser height shall be 7 3/4 inches (196mm). The riser shall be measured vertically between leading edges of the adjacent treads. The greatest riser height within any flight of stairs shall not exceed the smallest by more than 3/8 inch (9.5mm).

R311.5.3.2 Tread depth. The minimum tread depth shall be 10 inches (254mm). The tread depth shall be measured horizontally between the vertical planes of the foremost projection of adjacent treads and at a right angle to the tread's leading edge. The greatest tread depth within any flight of stairs shall not exceed the smallest by more than 3/8 inch (9.5mm). Winder treads shall have a minimum tread...

R311.5.3.3 Profile. ...A nosing not less than 3/4 inch (19mm) but not more than 1 1/4 inch (32mm) shall be provided on stairways with solid risers...

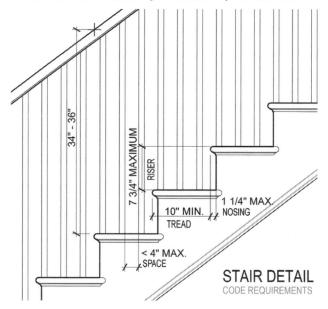

34" - 36"

7 3/4" MAXIMUM

RISER

1 1/4" MAX.
NOSING

10" MIN.
TREAD

< 4" MAX.
SPACE

STAIR DETAIL
CODE REQUIREMENTS

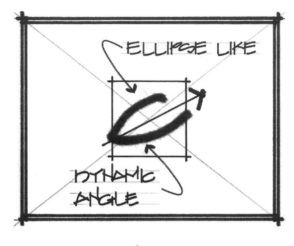

ELLIPSE LIKE

DYNAMIC
ANGLE

CHOIR

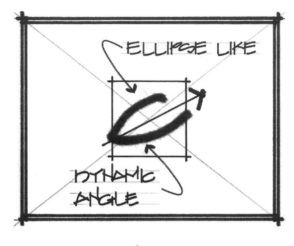

C IS FOR CHOIR

Designing and building architecture is somewhat like conducting a choir. When one person sings it can be beautiful, but with a choir a talented group is brought together for one cause, to make a harmonized declaration. In the field of architecture, a group of people with various specialties collaborate and make their own harmonized declaration—a building. This choir can have many members: architect, interior designer, landscape architect, structural engineer, mechanical engineer, audiovisual consultant, client, owner's representative, contractor, concrete workers, masons, steel fabricators, framers, insulation installers, drywallers, plumbers, electricians, plaster workers, millworkers, cabinet makers, heating, ventilation, and air conditioning experts, roofers, landscape crew, painters, local government agencies, the mortgage lender, loan processors, lawyers, and banks. All have to work together if the project is to run

Different architectural elements can be brought into harmony when linked together: a colonnade, slate roof, and shingle facade. Architect Jean Nouvel put mechanical stainless steel panels with thousands of shutters on the Institut du Monde Arabe. The shutters are of various shapes and sizes. They synchronize using photovoltaics to open and close in response to changing daylight conditions. The entire facade is composed of these panels. As a unified whole, it resembles an Arabian textile or rug.

smoothly, avoid delays, and stay within budget. Being an architect means managing and coordinating the many talented and specialized people that work with you and for you to make a building.

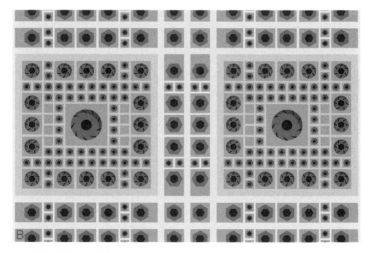

A detail view of the shutters.

This stone wall is made of similar elements, each depending on the other for support. The lintel above the window bears the weight of the stones just as the architect supports the work of other professionals. One stone is unremarkable, but a well-made wall is harmonious.

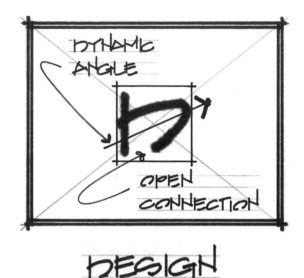

DYNAMIC ANGLE

OPEN CONNECTION

DESIGN

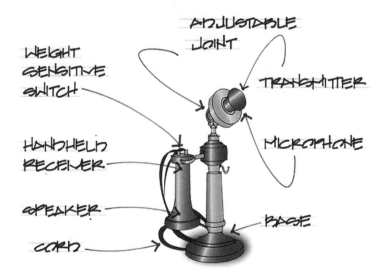

WEIGHT SENSITIVE SWITCH

ADJUSTABLE JOINT

TRANSMITTER

HANDHELD RECEIVER

MICROPHONE

SPEAKER

CORD

BASE

D IS FOR DESIGN

An architect designs buildings and collaborates in their construction. That sounds pretty straightforward. Design implies a kind of thoughtful planning relative to a set of parameters. Those parameters are called the "program" and are generated by the client. The program is a set of needs and desires for a project. The architect might design every part of a building: floor plans, exterior elevations, interior elevations, fittings, fixtures, and even furniture. He collaborates by providing supporting documents used in construction as well as performing site observation. He also coordinates a myriad of professionals and documents in the process. Design is an integral part of architecture, but contrary to popular thought it is only a small portion of what an architect does.

More generally, design is applied in the creation of everyday items like vacuum cleaners, sneakers, printers, headphones, telephones, silverware, furniture, automobiles, airplanes, trains, and of course buildings. Contrary to popular perception, design is a dynamic and time-consuming process that rarely reaches completion. Even when a product is on store shelves, the creators are probably busy working at the next model, and the consumer is consistently drawn in by new and improved versions of the product. The telephone is a perfect example. From telegraph to smart phone, this product has

Nine iterations for a front door of an early twentieth-century row house.

evolved continuously; the next best thing is just around the corner. Likewise, even after an extensive construction project the client is often thinking about another home, addition, renovation, office building, school, or skyscraper. And just as a client may never be done building, good design requires constant change in pursuit of an optimal solution.

Design is an iterative process. The architect will change his mind many times as the design evolves; the client will do the same. During the contract and bidding phase the overall design may stay the same, but smaller elements will be massaged based on price. Once the building is under way, changes are made for a number of reasons; the contractor may not have followed the drawings and specifications, the budget may be shrinking, or costs may have been managed improperly. Inevitably, design items are removed from the scope or altered to bring down cost. The architect might decide to change something after completion, or the client may be unhappy when she sees something unexpected. From beginning to end, changes are an integral part of the design process.

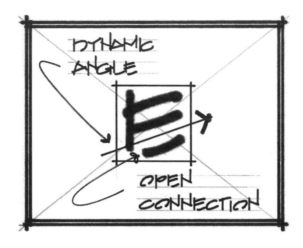

DYNAMIC
ANGLE

OPEN
CONNECTION

EGO

E IS FOR EGO

Good criticism isn't personal. Early in my career a boss pulled me aside and said, "You need broader shoulders." His comment was in response to the way he saw me react to criticism of my work in a meeting. My boss was right. I was sensitive, reacted poorly, and left the meeting without recognizing the value of a co-worker's insights. I had managed to get through my design courses in college without learning an important lesson. Being able to hear and use criticism is essential for architects. Humility is not surrender.

The studio course that most architecture students take involves long hours and hard work. It simulates the design process architects experience in practice. It is a hands-on environment where the young architect learns the tools of the trade. It is also here that he or she hones critical skills in design thinking. Part of this experience involves critiques or reviews. It is a chance for a professor or group of critics to review a student's process, progress, and finished work. It is one of the most memorable, stressful, and, sometimes, humiliating parts of an architect's education. I've seen more than one person leave a review in tears.

Making architecture is very personal. Every architect runs the programmatic elements through his or her own design filter. The outcome is a solution to a design problem that comes from individual experience and inclination. The process puts emotions, ideas, and preferences "out there" for criticism. It is personal. Good criticism is enlightening if it doesn't break you.

Humpty Dumpty sat on a wall,
Humpty Dumpty had a great fall;
All the king's horses, and all the king's men,
Couldn't put Humpty together again.

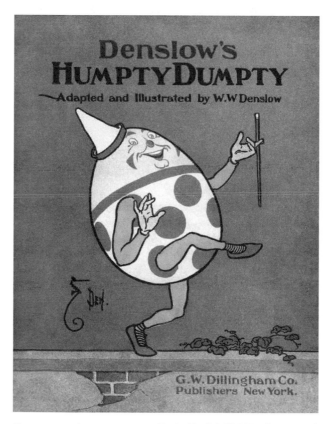

Humpty was a large cannon used in the English Civil War (1642–1649). It was dislodged from a wall and destroyed. The nursery rhyme, which came later, describes an egg that fell from a wall, never to be reassembled. Egos are like eggs; they can be crushed. A good architect has to be able to pull herself up and put herself back together again after a fall.

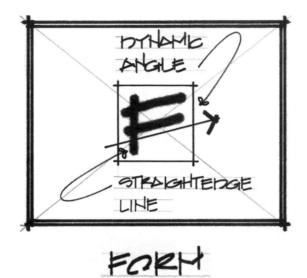

DYNAMIC
ANGLE

STRAIGHTEDGE
LINE

FORM

F IS FOR FORM

The phrase "form follows function" is associated with Louis Sullivan, a late nineteenth-/ early twentieth-century architect. Sullivan believed the form of a building should be determined by what goes on inside. In other words, function comes first. Later, modern architects adopted this same ideology and added the notion that buildings should be simplified to eliminate all ornament, allowing clarity of form and function never before seen in architecture. The phrase "form follows function" established a fundamental principle of design. In this view, regardless of whether one is designing a stadium, house, shoe, automobile, airplane, bike, or utensil, form is determined by function.

But sometimes function follows form. In other words, the form of a building is primary to function. This is a more contemporary concept. In the mid 1900s Mies van der Rohe created stripped-down, austere architecture that fit a modernist ideology, but these were simple boxes that could house any function. Even though he was associated with functionalism, his buildings were an alternative way of thinking about architecture, putting the form of a building ahead of the function. A building's overall form could be considered its most critical aspect; what happens on the inside is important, but secondary. Architects like Coop Himmelblau use the same ideology as Mies but in a more radical way. Their work is not simply streamlined boxes, but extreme shapes and configurations that make form the primary objective. From modernism to postmodernism to deconstructivism to blobitecture, creating the iconic figure is the intention. What's important here is not that one ideology is correct but that the architect is free to consider both.

But make no mistake: an architect designs for a client. She must work with the client to develop the form the client wants and the function he needs. The client will not look over the architect's shoulder every day, but at each meeting the client has the power to approve or veto the direction the architect has taken. Of course, an architect is hired for a reason: she is considered an expert. It's the job of an architect to help the client see the endgame and know the proper direction for the project. If a client is unwilling to budge, the architect has a choice: compromise or give up the commission.

It's worth noting that a bizarre building may be just what the client wants to attract attention to his business or himself. The shape may look nonfunctional, but it may in fact work perfectly for that reason. Alternatively, a client may want a completely drab design in which function is the driving force. The architect and client are paired in a deliberate way through the interview process. Hopefully, the architect's style and client's sensibilities match well from the start.

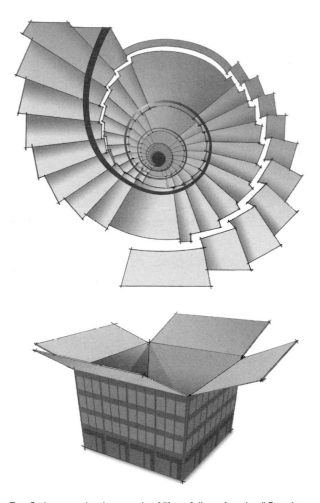

Top: Stairs are a classic example of "form follows function." Function—ascent and descent—is the driving force of their design. Here the form is a spiraling vertical riser and horizontal tread that accommodate that movement. Bottom: This cardboard box is an example of "function follows form." Form is the driving force of design. Like Mies's modern volumes, its form is generic, but elegant in its simplicity. Its purpose is to hold anything. Its shape will not change to accommodate the function.

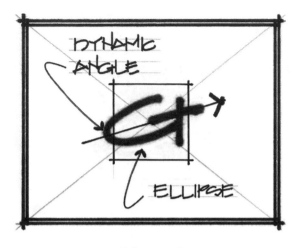

DYNAMIC
ANGLE

ELLIPSE

GRAVITY

G IS FOR GRAVITY

The gravitational force exerted by an object is a function of its mass. Our planet is huge relative to its inhabitants, and therefore exerts a large gravitational force on those of us who dwell on it. Our planet revolves around the enormous sun, and the smaller moon revolves around our earth. The solar system and our universe work the same way, and gravity holds it all together. When balls are dropped from a tower in Pisa, as Galileo may have done about 400 years ago, they fall. When an apple fell from a tree onto Sir Isaac Newton it gave him an idea: all things are governed by the same gravitational force. Gravity is a fact of life and affects everything we do and make, including architecture.

The first architectural forms came from the realization that we must hold something up (against the forces of gravity) in order to create a space that will protect our body, friends, family, and belongings from the elements. We've come a long way since Laugier's drawing of the primitive hut that describes an idealized notion of what the first dwellings looked like: contrast that with today's mind-bending architectural structures. But it all started somewhere. Beyond primitive cave dwellings and pyramids, the first buildings took their form from necessity. Pitched roofs, posts, mud bricks, and thatch were used to create space inside and keep water out. These simple structures evolved into highly substantial edifices, such as those on the acropolis in Greece, the language of which was elaborated over time. Buildings evolved into more complex structures as people sought light and mastered materials and gravitational forces. We see this in the great cathedrals of the Middle Ages. Buildings became about what could be, not what had to be. Structural gymnastics slowly became reality with the flying buttress of the medieval cathedral and, during the industrial revolution, the steel and glass of the Crystal Palace. Elisha Otis demonstrated his invention, the safety elevator, at the New York world's fair of 1854. With its help, building heights were no longer limited by a lack of vertical transportation. The steel skyscrapers of Louis Sullivan surpassed masonry structures like the Monadnock Building in Chicago by Burnham & Root. Glass replaced thick opaque walls. Building themes changed—from small windows and heavy materials to all windows and lightweight structural skeletons. From predictable forms to anything goes. Gravity never went away, but minds and new materials were slowly mastering it. The architectural boldness we see from Frank Gehry, Santiago Calatrava, or Rem Koolhaas is possible because advances in technology allowed them almost complete freedom of expression, despite gravitational forces. Technology, skills of the general contractor and tradesmen, advanced materials, and precision machinery all have advanced the possibilities of building form and height. The future of architectural structures is anyone's guess, but gravity is certainly not slowing it down.

A famous image from Marc-Antoine Laugier's *Essay on Architecture*, published in 1753.

The China Central Television headquarters building in Beijing, designed by Rem Koolhaas. This building has an unusual shape and a sky-high, death-defying cantilever.

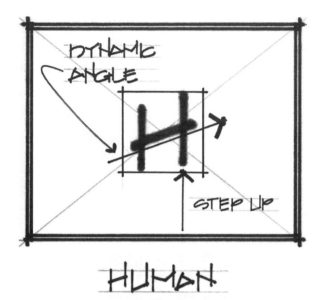

DYNAMIC
ANGLE

STEP UP

HUMAN

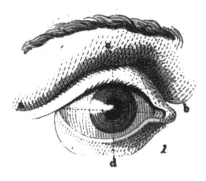

H IS FOR HUMAN

The buildings that clothe us also reflect us. We make clothing to fit our bodies and we make buildings to fit our lives. That is, architecture expresses how we think, behave, work, and live. It communicates our divisions and our common ground. Whether it's a cottage or a mansion, corner store or shopping mall, school or skyscraper, office building or courthouse, prison or stadium, buildings reflect who we are, who we believe ourselves to be, what we want and what we need.

Architecture is made to fit our bodies or exploit our size. Throughout history it has also been described in relation to our anatomy. For example, the cubit, an ancient measuring device, was originally determined by the length of one's forearm. In fact, many measurements originated as the lengths of various parts of the human body (e.g., foot, palm, thumb, finger).

The architect should understand human nature and society. How people behave is a big part of what goes into designing a building. For example, in contemporary society, when people gather informally at someone's house they always seem to congregate in the kitchen, regardless of its size. It doesn't seem to matter that the house has a huge living room or screened-in porch; the guests always end up in the kitchen. That's important for an architect to know when his or her client asks for a small

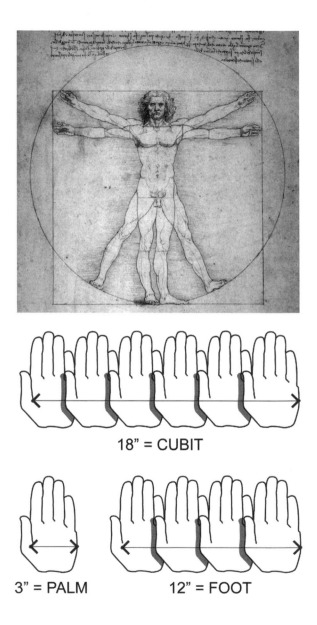

18" = CUBIT

3" = PALM

12" = FOOT

kitchen or walls that will impede gathering or traffic. Another example is the behavior of people at sporting events. The volume and weight of the attendees and the amount of motion they create when rooting for their favorite team are essential design considerations. The architect and structural engineer will, no doubt, examine these factors when designing the structural system for the stadium. Some stadiums even have courtrooms and jail cells to hold people who have become drunk and disorderly—now that's being responsive to the needs of human beings!

Top: Vitruvian man by Leonardo da Vinci. The drawing depicts proportional relationships developed by Vitruvius in his treatise *De architectura*. Bottom: Dimensional units have had a variety of sources throughout history. According to Vitruvius, 6 palms (a palm is the width of four fingers) equal a cubit and four palms equal a foot.

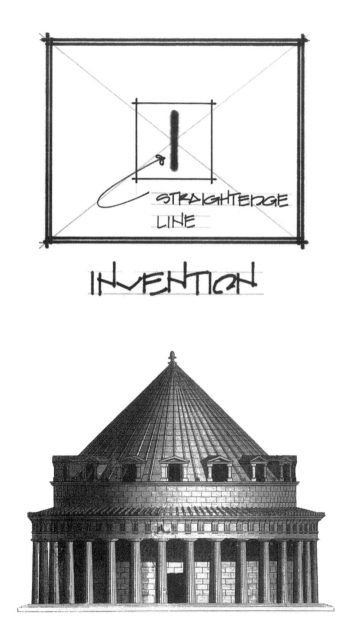

STRAIGHTEDGE
LINE

INVENTION

I IS FOR INVENTION

Many people consider the architect to be just a designer. But the architect does more than arrange lines and shapes in the form of a building. She conceives of something original. In this way, architects are inventors.

An inventor creates, out of necessity, something that does not already exist. There are three types of patents that can be filed with the United States Patent and Trademark Office: Utility, Design, and Plant. The architect may not be filing a patent, but she does create an object of utility, an invention. In a way every building, every house, every skyscraper, every thing an architect creates, if it's original and provides utility, is an invention. A building becomes something of an invention by virtue of the specific requirements of the client—the program. The architects does something for her client that her client can't usually do for himself: solve his programmatic needs through design. A building's utility lies in the unique function it embodies. A "thing" has the quality of utility when it is advantageous, useful, or valuable. When a building is designed well it typifies these qualities. An architect takes the program defined by the

The Odeon of Pericles at Athens, in this 1849 reconstruction in J. G. Heck's *Complete Encyclopedia of Illustration*, is a simplistic form with an inventive roof and dormers.

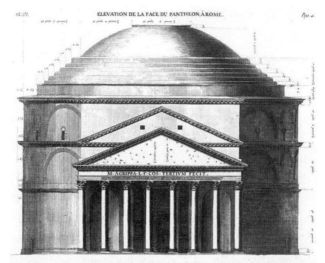

client and designs a space, series of spaces, or object that defines space. That object is useful to the client because it is profitable or beneficial to him in some way. Just as the inventor solves a problem with a new product, the architect solves her client's programmatic requirements with a new building. In the process she may also create new ways of solving problems that can be inventions in themselves.

Top: The Pantheon in Rome was rebuilt in 126 AD by order of the emperor Hadrian. This ingenious marvel has inspired similar works around the world. It is the largest unreinforced concrete dome anywhere. The concrete rings, on the outside of the domed roof, help reinforce against outward stress. Bottom: An interior view of the dome. Invisibly to the eye, the shell thickness tapers toward the top. The aggregate used in the concrete gets smaller and lighter on the way up, and the recessed coffers and oculus also diminish its weight.

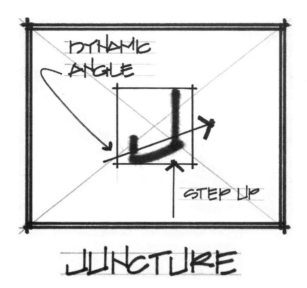

DYNAMIC
ANGLE

STEP UP

JUNCTURE

J IS FOR JUNCTURE

Architecture is the art of putting materials together. How materials are put together affects the strength, weather resistance, and aesthetics of a building. In some areas of the world, providing shelter is the most critical component of architecture. In others it's wind or seismic forces that drive decisions. Water is a building's most insidious enemy. If it gets in, the building will rot slowly from the inside out. If wind takes off parts of a building, they become flying projectiles. An earthquake can shake a building to partial or complete destruction. There is a delicate tension in architecture in making a building strong but not too cumbersome; making a building weather resistant while allowing enough of the outside in to enjoy our surroundings; connecting materials soundly but making the details subtle or beautiful. The assemblage of a building's parts is essential to safety and comfort. But it also conveys elegance and sophistication. Most people overlook the meeting of materials, but to the trained eye it reveals the dedication and thought that goes into making beautiful things. Elegance can be found in the unseen details of construction, in the way a window sits in a wall, the meeting of materials on a facade, the assemblage of structural parts, or the millwork details of cabinetry. The multitude of junctures throughout a building constitutes one element of its success.

An image created from Julius Shulman's famous photograph of the Stahl House in Los Angeles. The house was designed by Pierre Koenig. The delicate junctures are subdued and minimal to accentuate the incredible view.

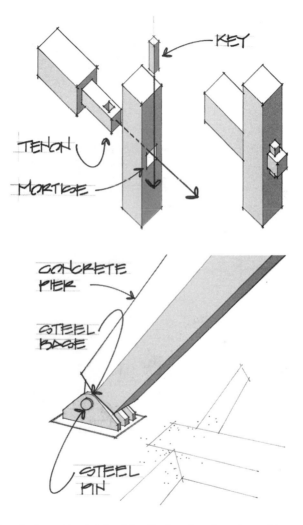

KEY

TENON

MORTISE

CONCRETE PIER

STEEL BASE

STEEL PIN

Top: An isometric sketch of the timeless keyed-mortise-and-tenon connection found in arts and crafts–style furniture. Variations of the joint can be seen in millwork and heavy timber construction. Bottom: A detail from the Milwaukee Art Museum by Santiago Calatrava. It demonstrates elegance and minimalism with incredible strength.

DYNAMIC
ANGLE

STRAIGHTEDGE
LINE

KEVIN BACON

K IS FOR KEVIN BACON

Most of us have heard the phrase "six degrees of separation"—the notion that we are all connected to each other by a maximum of six intermediate relationships. You've probably also heard the phrase "six degrees of Kevin Bacon" (the idea that any actor can be linked to Kevin Bacon in a chain of association by six connections or less, based on the many movies in which Mr. Bacon has appeared). When I was in graduate school, I went to hear a lecture by a man named Edmund Bacon, who happens to have been the father of Kevin Bacon the actor. The elder Mr. Bacon was an architect, teacher, and writer; he worked for the City of Philadelphia Planning Commission for many years and taught at the University of Pennsylvania. During the lecture I attended he said, "It's in the doing that the idea comes." That simple phrase has meant a lot to me as an architect. That's because Mr. Bacon was saying that nothing comes free and you've got to work hard to make things happen. When you are working on any project, from the design of a home to the creation of a new product, big ideas rarely just materialize out of thin air. There are certainly stories of people who were just sitting around and had a great idea, but it's not the typical experience. Rather, great ideas mature from the smaller ones that emerge as we do hard work. Ideas build on themselves, evolve, and reciprocate. Mr. Bacon meant that during hard work, big ideas slowly build to a crescendo or take us in new and sometimes better directions. For an architect, hard work entails writing, sketching, drawing, drafting, model making, collaboration, and, finally, making lots of revisions to something before it goes to construction. Good ideas are earned through hard work and an open mind.

Frank Furness was a well-known Victorian-era Philadelphia architect. His work was prolific and unique. Unfortunately, many of the buildings he designed have been demolished. His designs were mannerist, powerful, and bold. His work was an early gateway for architects challenging conventional style. His Pennsylvania Academy of Fine Arts and University of Pennsylvania Library still stand in Philadelphia. This is a photograph of the University of Pennsylvania Library taken in 1900.

The Provident Life & Trust Company Building, completed in 1879 and also designed by Furness.

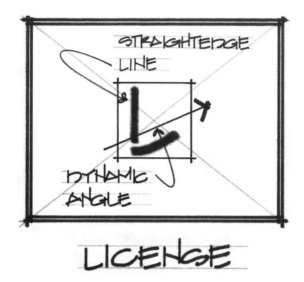

LICENSE

L IS FOR LICENSE

There are software architects, information architects, systems architects, as well as the architects of a campaign or event. Technically, one should not call oneself an architect of buildings without being an RA (Registered Architect). The word "architect" is highly regarded as a designation within the profession, but in recent years it has come to be used more and more loosely by people in other fields to describe work that has nothing to do with the design of buildings.

The path to becoming a building architect can be quite protracted. Getting into college is the first hurdle. This can be challenging; regardless of the size of the university, many architecture programs are small and selective. To get an accredited architecture degree in the United States can take anywhere from five to eight years. Each state has its own requirements for licensing an architect. If you're in a state that requires NAAB (National Architectural Accreditation Board) accreditation, you'll most likely be enrolling in the Intern Development Program (IDP) after you finish school. The IDP is a program run by the National Council of Architectural Registration Boards (NCARB). It's a continuation of the education started in college during which you keep a record of your experience as an intern. It takes a minimum of three years, usually longer. Following completion, you're eligible for the Architectural Registration Examination (ARE). The ARE is a national computerized exam consisting of seven parts. You are considered eligible for licensure once you've passed all seven parts. Your NCARB record becomes a passport to licensure in other states. Each state has its own schedule of fees and requirements for maintaining a license. It's quite a bureaucracy, but it does serve a purpose. Once licensed, you'll also be eligible to join various professional organizations like the American Institute of Architects (AIA) or obtain designations like LEED certification.

Some states require a license to practice architecture, while others do not. I have a number of friends who waited many years to get their license because they simply didn't need it in the office where they worked. I have others who had a tough time passing the test and took years to earn the title "Registered Architect." Whether or not you need that license will depend on your position in a firm, level of responsibility, local requirements for signing and stamping drawings, and personal goals.

Salaries also tend to get bumped up slightly when an architect gains the designation, but architects' salaries are typically less than those of other licensed professionals (doctors, lawyers).

Reference: "Guide to Architecture Schools," Association of Collegiate Schools of Architecture, July 30, 2007.

A fictitious architect's stamp. This stamp is embossed. The architect embosses or ink-stamps drawings, specifications, and reports to certify their authenticity. The stamp is required when submitting work for review by local or state authorities.

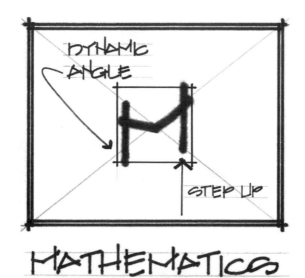

DYNAMIC
ANGLE

STEP UP

MATHEMATICS

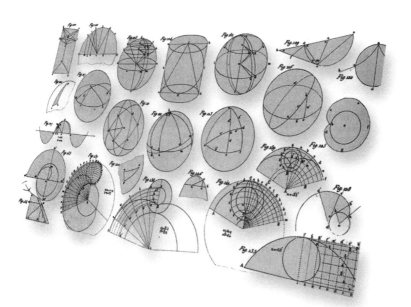

M IS FOR MATHEMATICS

Architecture is a business of dimensions, measurements, and calculations. It involves mathematics. I've been told more than once that the only reason someone decided not to study architecture is because they weren't good in math. Do you have to be a mathematician to be an architect? No. Should you be decent at math? Yes. One of the ways a building is described is in mathematical terms: dimensions and calculations. The architect must have a firm grasp of how a building is numerically described and how calculations affect the integrity of the building's structural system. An architectural engineer will assist with specific calculations that determine structural systems and load-bearing elements. Mathematics and physics are necessary to ensure that buildings stand up. The design of some buildings involves complex mathematical calculations and challenges architects on their grasp of physics and math. The architecture student studies these subjects because she needs to understand the principles behind them.

Good design decisions depend on understanding the natural world, physics and materials. Mathematics is the convention we use to quantify the limits of man-made objects. If you are interested in becoming an architect, you will need to have some skill in math. Your competency will be critical to passing structural

courses in college and making informed decisions as a professional. However, the architect can hire professionals for help when solving the complex mathematics of structural systems.

John Roebling, a civil engineer, designed the Brooklyn Bridge, using mathematical calculations to make the bridge significantly stronger than it needed to be in 1883. Today it can handle six lanes of vehicular traffic and a walkway for pedestrians. The bridge represents the convergence of engineering and architectural intelligence in an iconic American structure. Serving structural requirements with a neo-Gothic aesthetic, the bridge also marks a new era of suburbanization in America when transportation began to drive public works.

N IS FOR NARRATIVE

Architecture can tell a narrative by virtue of form, material, and experience. Often architecture looks like what it is and does. Robert Venturi coined the phrase "duck" for a building that makes a bold, recognizable figurative statement through form: that is, a building that looks like what it is in an overt way. An example might be the Kansas City Public Library. Its parking garage is made to look like books on a bookshelf. The Longaberger Basket Company Headquarters in Newark, Ohio, belongs to a basket manufacturer. That building looks like a giant basket! In these examples the association of function and form is so obvious that it might be considered overdone. Architects like to call these "one-liners." The trick in architecture is to add meaning with subtlety and finesse. Thoughtfully considered materials and form enhance the experience of a building if done well.

When I think of architecture that tells a story in more subtle ways, I think of Frank Lloyd Wright's Guggenheim Museum in New York City. It tells a story from the outside about how people move through the spiraling galleries on the inside. The Pompidou Center in Paris, by Renzo Piano and Richard Rogers, tells a color-coded story from the exterior about its mechanical inner workings. Each color of the exterior refers to a type of mechanical system on the inside: green for water, blue for air, yellow for electricity, red for transportation. Rogers's Lloyd's Building tells a story of strength with its famous stainless steel facade, and suggests the movement of people and machinery on the interior with the spiraling stair towers and exposed mechanical systems. The stainless steel facade is a message about Lloyd's impenetrable and dependable business position.

A classical facade or colonnade tells a story about formality, judgment, stateliness, or ritual. An office building or factory may tell a less interesting story through repeating patterns and windows on the exterior that echo the redundant tasks of machines and employees within. Religious structures often tell the story of thoughts and prayers offered to the heavens, or how the building's immense height and stained glass have somehow captured part of God's majesty and made it available to mankind.

Sometimes buildings look like the story they embody; they are a narrative of function. Other times they look nothing like what they are. This might be the case

Top: Frank Lloyd Wright's Guggenheim Museum in New York City from the street. Bottom: A view of the museum from the interior as people pass along the large ascending ramps and view artwork along the wall.

with buildings that have been renovated for new functions. Old schoolhouses, churches, or barns became homes or restaurants; factory warehouses became loft apartments, artists' studios, or galleries. Buildings don't have to look like what they are to be successful, but subtleties in style, material, and form can strengthen the architect's message.

The temple of Zeus at Olympia.

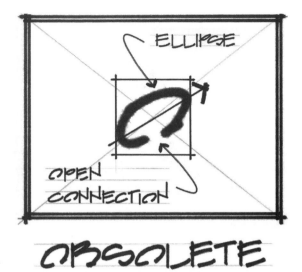

ELLIPSE

OPEN
CONNECTION

OBSOLETE

O IS FOR OBSOLETE

Pyramids were built as tombs for pharaohs. We don't have pharaohs anymore. We do have leaders, but we don't bury them inside giant monuments (with occasional more modest exceptions, like Grant's tomb). Building types become obsolete for a variety of reasons. Society changes, wealth spreads, and technology advances. Cave dwellings, castles, forts, cenotaphs, catacombs, telegraph stations, carriage houses, and drive-in movie theaters are all obsolete. Today we make home theaters instead of drive-ins, McMansions instead of castles, and office towers instead of forts.

Not too long ago, architects used slide rules for math and calipers to check measurements. Now they use digital calculators and scales. Pencils, erasers, templates, compasses, triangles, tape, paper, and parallel rules are still used, but less frequently than they once were. Hand lettering is a lost art and not many architects reach for the T-square these days. Large drafting tables used to be the furniture of choice for architects. Today the architect can draft on a laptop without a desk. In the first office I worked in, we made models from balsa wood and drew with ink pens. Today we hire model makers that cut plastic parts with lasers and use software to make visual 3D models that could pass for photographs.

The architect's job is to create something unique. Today we have books and websites with vast arrays of "exclusive" designs for homes and prefabricated buildings of every kind. We have choices because designers have given us affordable options. The construction industry employs architects and designers, but they also hire project managers, construction managers, owners' representatives, and a wide variety of building and legal professionals who can get buildings built quickly and at a better price. It's all about efficiency. Is it just a matter of time until the architect is obsolete?

Hugh Ferriss was an architect and delineator. Today, the computer has rendered his techniques obsolete. His hand-drawn work was a high point in the history of architectural illustration. He possessed a strong working knowledge of the artistic use of value (the spectrum of light to dark). This rendering of the New York Daily News Building was done by Ferriss in 1930.

In 1922 Ferriss was commissioned by an architect to create drawings that described new zoning laws in New York City. These laws made obsolete certain kinds of building practices, such as buildings that blocked the vicinity's access to sunlight. Stepping buildings back as they gained elevation allowed for more sunlight on the ground below. Not only did Ferriss illustrate the new laws, but his drawings became famous as a new and lasting vision for skyscrapers. This is a replication of one of his well-known drawings.

ELLIPSE

DYNAMIC
ANGLE

PROPORTION

13'-0"

20'-0"

7'-0"

SMALL DOOR

LARGE DOOR

P IS FOR PROPORTION

Proportion is the relationship of one thing to another. Architects like to use the word "scale" which they apply in an obscure but appropriate way, to refer to the sizing of elements to exploit everyday human experience. For example, when people see a door, they expect it to be about 7 feet high. When an architect designs a building with 20-foot-high doors, he expects people to respond according to their experience with typical doors. If the building is very large, the 20-foot doors will look the appropriate size from far away. Once a person gets up close, the doors might look right for the building, but surprisingly large for a human being. Or the architect might manipulate the scale of a large building by making seeming 20-foot doors out of false fixed panels, with a more normal-sized working door at their base. With this he achieves the illusion of gigantic working doors that look proportional to the building but completely overwhelm the visitor close up—a building for giants! The architect must know how to size all the parts of a building so that people will respond to the building according to his intent.

A human-scaled door juxtaposed with a monumental one.

Egyptian pyramids, Greek temples, and Roman buildings like the Pantheon or Coliseum promoted power and authority by proportional manipulations. The scale of these buildings, relative to the people who used them, was enormous. Later, Gothic and Renaissance architects did the same with cathedrals and palaces. And still later, as modernism expanded its foothold and detail was replaced by large blank facades, buildings used the large curtain wall to create superhuman scale. Clearly defined forms on a massive scale do the same thing that the buildings of the Egyptians or Greeks did in their time: assert power, authority, or dominance over the natural world.

Jean Nouvel used a curtain wall in the ambiguously scaled elevations of the Institut du Monde Arabe in Paris and the colorful Agbar tower in Barcelona. I. M. Pei's modern glass John Hancock Tower in Boston looms over the significantly smaller, older, and beautifully detailed Trinity Church by H. H. Richardson. The tower deliberately reflects the church in its huge expanse of glass; it is a stark study in proportional difference. We see the same effect in Norman Foster's Hearst Tower in New York City or Swiss Re Building (the "Gherkin") in London. Rem Koolhaas used undulating scaleless volumes for his Seattle Public Library and massive inverted horseshoe-shaped cantilevers for his CCTV tower in China. Any discernible relationship to human scale is obliterated by the countless rings that vertically climb César Pelli's Petronas Towers of Kuala Lumpur, Malaysia.

At the other end of the spectrum, architects like Frank Lloyd Wright created buildings with proportion that matched human scale. The ceilings of buildings such as Taliesen West or Fallingwater feel comfortable and even low. The interior materials, like wood and cork, lend themselves to repose and warmth. Le Corbusier developed his own "modular" system of proportion based on the human figure, intended to make better places for people to live. He did this with elevated buildings, roof gardens, and open floor plans. His success was debatable. However, his work paved the way for modern residential architects like Richard Neutra whose work was austere but well scaled, sunny and comfortable. The proportion of a building to its user, its scale, is one of the architect's most important tools of expression.

The Martin Luther King Jr. Library in Washington, D.C., by Mies van der Rohe is deceivingly monumental. (A) This human figure looks as though he could be the proper size for the building, but he is not. (B) This human figure is the proper size. The figure is approximately 6 feet tall. The height of the first-floor window wall behind is approximately 18 feet.

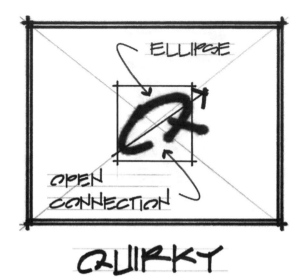

ELLIPSE

OPEN
CONNECTION

QUIRKY

Q IS FOR QUIRKY

Quirk is an architectural term. It's a small V-shaped channel placed in a surface to give visual relief. A quirk casts a shadow that makes a surface or object more pronounced. Architects are quirky. They like to wear black. They might be seen sporting plaid sweaters, suspenders, or bow ties. Many architects look as if they buy their clothes from the same preppy outfitter. They like glasses with bold rims too. Le Corbusier, Eero Saarinen, Philip Johnson, Daniel Libeskind, Peter Eisenman, and many more wear (or wore) glasses.

Le Corbusier sometimes painted in the nude. Frank Lloyd Wright refused to add reinforcing to the cantilevers at Fallingwater just to spite an engineer. Wright customarily wore a cape and beret. Oscar Niemeyer, a centenarian, married his secretary just before he turned 99. The architects of Coop Himmelblau have been known to draw with their eyes closed. Leon Krier and Lebbeus Woods, both architects, would rather draw than make buildings. Rem Koolhaas swims every day. And Louis Kahn mastered a life of quirkiness—where to even begin?

There are also lots of quirky buildings in the world. Frank Furness challenged convention with his muscular and peculiar style. Antoni Gaudí took things a step further and made truly unusual architecture. His buildings are nothing if not aberrational. He began work on one

In 1978, Frank Gehry did something extraordinary to his home in Santa Monica, California. Taking what was a very ordinary two-story, single-family gambrel-roofed house in a suburban neighborhood, he stripped it back to its framing and rafters, then wrapped the old structure with corrugated metal siding, plywood, glass, and chain-link fencing, turning the house into a piece of sculpture.

of his most famous buildings, the church of the Sagrada Família in Barcelona, in 1883, and spent the rest of his life designing it. More than eighty-five years after his death, the cathedral is still being built. Frank Gehry's Guggenheim Museum in Bilbao, Spain, resembles a building that was dismantled and then reassembled improperly. The architecture of Santiago Calatrava is as otherworldly as are the drawings of Lebbeus Woods, whose drawings, sketches, and models depict buildings and spaces that could appear in the *Star Wars* movies. Oscar Niemeyer designs buildings shaped like spaceships, salad bowls, and eyeballs. Shin Takamatsu's futuristic buildings look like machines mixed with DNA. Coop Himmelblau's work on Falkestrasse in Vienna is one of the most unique additions in the world. A small structure sitting on top of a traditional Viennese building, it functions as a meeting room for a law practice, but the design defies all laws.

In 1949 Philip Johnson designed one of his most famous works for one of his most famous clients—himself. The house Johnson designed is called the Glass House. Although Johnson was enigmatic in many ways, he chose to live in a house that was literally transparent.

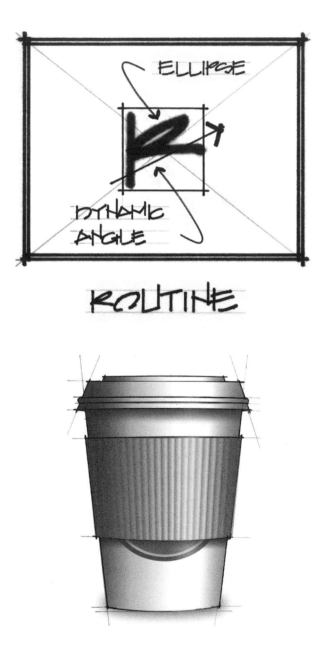

ELLIPSE

DYNAMIC ANGLE

ROUTINE

R IS FOR ROUTINE

What is the architect's daily routine? He does many jobs in an office. First, he makes presentations to clients and participates in competitions to secure work. At the beginning of any project several levels of site documentation and analysis are necessary, such as site plan reviews, property setback and zoning requirements, as well as other federal state and municipal limitations. Next, the architect develops a schematic design to present the client with an initial conceptual layout for the building. Eventually he creates more detailed drawings with greater accuracy. The architect starts to research materials and double-checks code and zoning compliance issues. Input from other professionals is sought regarding structural, mechanical, electrical, and audiovisual matters. Once the design has been approved, he develops construction documents on his own or with a team. These include a complete set of plans, elevations, wall sections, and details as well as written specifications that define every material choice and related building information. This drawing package can be as small as one or two pages or as large as hundreds of pages, depending

Architects drink a lot of coffee. In the United States, coffee drinkers average 3.1 cups per day.

on the cost of the project, the number of professionals involved, the scale, and the level of detail required. At this point, other professionals involved in the project work closely with the architect to provide information that support his work. The architect coordinates everything. Once construction documents are complete, the project is bid and negotiated. Eventually a construction firm is awarded the project. The architect performs site observation and participates or runs site meetings. He also supports the contractor in the field with clarification documents during construction. The length of the journey and the number of people involved varies greatly depending on the type of project. The architect does all of these things and more, at any given time of his working day. The day-to-day work can be monotonous, but there are plenty of opportunities for finding ongoing challenge and enjoyment within the daily routine.

Architects today have an extensive architectural playbook, but the Romans did not. Their daily routine was immersed in the mastery and practice of a distinct and limited architectural language. The five classical orders had rules concerning proportions, details, and use. Each column had a distinct base, shaft, capital, and entablature. From left to right, top to bottom are the Tuscan, Doric, Ionic, Ionic detail, Corinthian, and Composite capitals and entablatures.

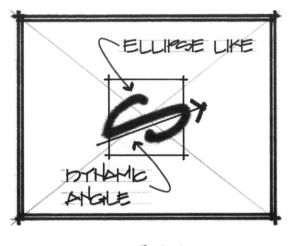

ELLIPSE LIKE

DYNAMIC
ANGLE

STYLE

S IS FOR STYLE

Style means a label, a kind, a variety, a class, a genre, or even a brand. Branded items are ubiquitous, from drinks to automobiles. Architecture can be like a brand: mansions like Versace, shore houses like Ralph Lauren, cowboy ranches like Levi, etc. Like other produced goods, architecture comes in many styles. This reflects the many ways people have discovered—since the beginning of time—to make places for other people to live and work. Sometimes buildings are highly stylized and reveal exactly the era in which they were built. The attention and detail they possess conveys an intentional message. Sometimes buildings look more generic. They could fit into many times and places and convey little about the designer's intent.

We usually make buildings look like what we want them to mean. Some styles are classified by their relationship to a past civilization like that of ancient Greece, Rome, or Egypt. Others are known by their origin in a particular philosophical or social era like the Renaissance, baroque, or Victorian. Still others were created as part of an architectural school or movement like the Bauhaus, De Stijl, or deconstructivism. Whatever the designation, most architecture can be classified, and those classifications become part of architectural history and theory. When it comes to making buildings, architects can choose a style. Some choose to work within an existing style, others create their own, still others are more eclectic, changing their style to meet the needs of different clients or a particular "brand" affiliation.

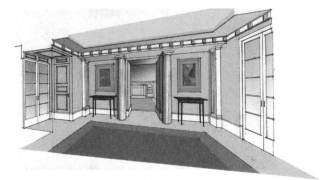

Stylistic elements are adaptable. Top: A western view of the Parthenon in Greece. Bottom: A sketch for a client who wanted to renovate his living room in the Greek revival style. Greek Doric columns, fluted pilasters, drywall soffits, new millwork, and a dentil molding were suggested.

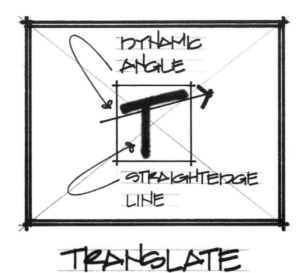

DYNAMIC
ANGLE

STRAIGHTEDGE
LINE

TRANSLATE

T IS FOR TRANSLATE

A painter takes a subject and translates it. Vincent van Gogh was a postimpressionist who had a command of color and an unusual way of using brushstrokes to define a subject. He said of his paintings that "my greatest desire is to reveal such inaccuracies, such deviations, revisions, alterations of reality, that they may be, well—lies if one pleases—but truer than the literal truth."[1] Van Gogh took a subject, interpreted it, and painted it. He wanted the end result to be "truer than the literal truth." He breathed new life into a "thing" by remaking it as a painting. In the process of creating a new work he made it uniquely meaningful through translation. This is what an architect does also.

An architect translates a user's vision into a built environment. Just as a translator takes the words of one person and makes them clear to another, the architect translates the desires of a client into a meaningful and useful object. The tools of the architect are imagination, words, drawings, and models. The architect uses them to generate her translation. The first client meeting should include a discussion of the program. This information encompasses everything the client wants. The architect takes the program and designs a building. If it's a home, the program includes the number of bathrooms, bedrooms, kitchen needs, number of garages, finishes,

1. Vincent van Gogh, letter to his brother Theo, July 1885.

fixtures, millwork, etc. If it's an industrial or commercial building it includes function, offices, delivery space, utility rooms, executive suites, meeting rooms, etc. In simple terms, the architect takes the program and finds a solution; the contractor takes this solution and, with labor and materials, turns it into a building. The architect infuses part of herself into a building through her unique translation. If it weren't so, every architect's work would look the same. As it stands, architects have been translating the program in unique ways since the first one was employed.

Like Van Gogh, the architect's goal is to take her subject, in this case the client, the site, and the program, interpret it, and translate that into a design. She can design something that is a literal translation of her subject or, like Van Gogh, make something that is "truer than the literal truth." In other words, the architect can design a building that doesn't just solve the programmatic requirements but exceeds the client's expectations, going beyond the program and enriching the experience of a place.

Top: Van Gogh's *Starry Night* shows that he saw the night as dynamic. The stars and moon shimmer, space swirls with motion. The hills and plant life roll through the painting, and everything writhes and glows. Bottom: Frank Lloyd Wright turned Edgar J. Kaufmann's wish for a home in Bear Run, Pennsylvania, into one of the most celebrated houses in America. Nestled into a hillside, it sits over a waterfall and cantilevers in many directions.

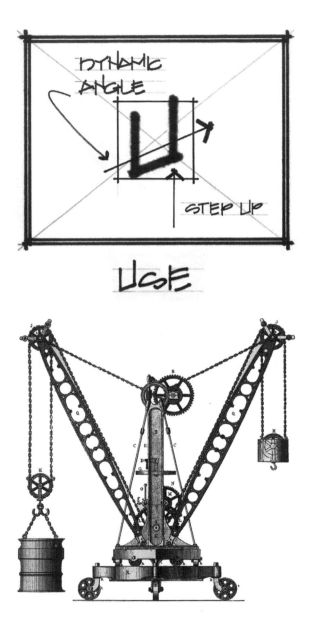

U IS FOR USE

Once, during a job interview, an architect asked me to name sixteen places where a residential home opens to the exterior. I could only name nine and thus received a less than desirable job offer. The question was unusual for a job interview but fundamental to the profession. Architecture is not all about creativity; it's also about knowing what a building needs to function properly. If a building isn't comfortable for work, people won't use it. A building's mechanical systems are critical to its operation. Knowing sixteen places where a residential home is open to the exterior is really about understanding how all the components work together to make the building usable.

Buildings require circulated air to maintain a suitable living and work environment. In damp environments it is also essential to keep moisture low, to prevent susceptible parts from swelling or rotting. For these reasons a building should have heating, ventilation, and usually air conditioning. Because all our modern amenities are electrical, a building also needs an extensive system of cables, outlets, conduits, and fuse boxes. It has mechanical systems and an intricate and cumbersome network of pipes, vents, ducts, devices, outlets, inlets, boilers, and pumps. It has audio/visual systems with thousands of wires, cables, speakers, televisions, telephones, and the like. All of these things run concealed within floors, ceilings, and walls without interfering with one another or the building's elements. Functional, well-placed building components and mechanical systems are critical to the building's comfort and use.

Just so you know: the sixteen places on a residential home that are open to the exterior are windows, doors, gable vent, ridge vent, cupola vent, soffit vent, boiler flue, plumbing vent, bathroom exhaust, wall-mounted hot water heater vent, foundation vent, range hood vent, dryer vent, masonry fireplace flue, gas fireplace vent, all varieties of foundation conduits, and I'm sure there are more …

The Georges Pompidou Center in Paris by Renzo Piano and Richard Rogers. The building is inside out. The exterior is clad in mechanical elements like ducts, conduits, and pipes as well as transportation and structural systems, thus increasing the amount of interior space that can be used for exhibitions.

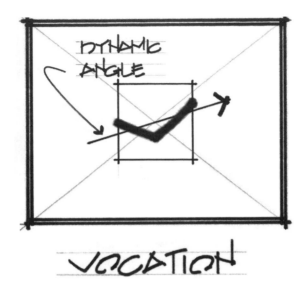

DYNAMIC ANGLE

VOCATION

V IS FOR VOCATION

A vocation is work for which an individual is particularly qualified. If you want to pursue architecture as a vocation, take stock before heading down the long road. You should be decent at math, but that's not all. You don't have to be an artist, but you should be able to sketch; sketching conveys ideas quickly and succinctly. Today, most architectural drawing is done on a computer, so drafting by hand might be considered obsolete. A few architects still prepare construction documents with pencil and parallel rule, but manual drafting is far more time-consuming when making changes. Sketching can be done with architectural software, but there really is no substitute for a quick sketch done by hand on a piece of paper or computer tablet, to convey an idea. If you can't draw well but would like to learn, this shouldn't deter you from becoming an architect. Sketching, like other skills, can be improved with practice.

To be a good architect, having a good command of language is critical. Words are one of the ways that architects convey information about building design. This underscores the architect's two roles as salesperson and writer. The architect has to be a good salesman. He must sell himself and his firm to get work. It's also the architect's job to convey on paper or a computer screen his ideas, intentions, details, and clarifications. So, secondly,

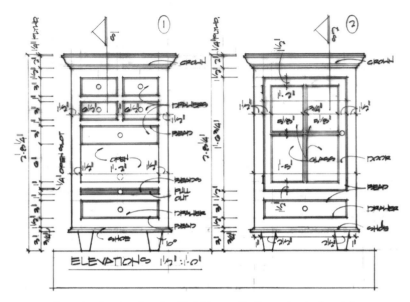

A construction drawing of a side table, used by the contractor for pricing and developing shop drawings.

he must be a good writer. The architect should be able to communicate his plans in sufficient detail that others can execute them accurately. It is the architect's job to work with all the many consultants, designers, contractors, lawyers, and clients with written and verbal efficiency. The architect generates and reviews contracts, meeting minutes, construction documents, clarification documents, change orders, etc. So if you have a gift for language it will definitely come in handy.

Creativity is also an important part of being an architect. Are you inventive? Imaginative? Such traits will help with a critical aspect of design—problem solving. Problem solving is about taking an idea and turning it into something real, like a building. It involves working through every aspect of a particular challenge through research, sketching, drawing, model making, and other modes of expression. Problem solving generates the ideas that eventually coalesce into a tangible thing.

There is no hard-and-fast rule for success. A person who is creative and good at drawing but poor in math and English might make a great architect. Another may be proficient in all four categories but never design anything significant. Beyond proficiency, there is motivation and discipline. This translates into being conscientious, which is indeed a requisite of success in the profession of architecture.

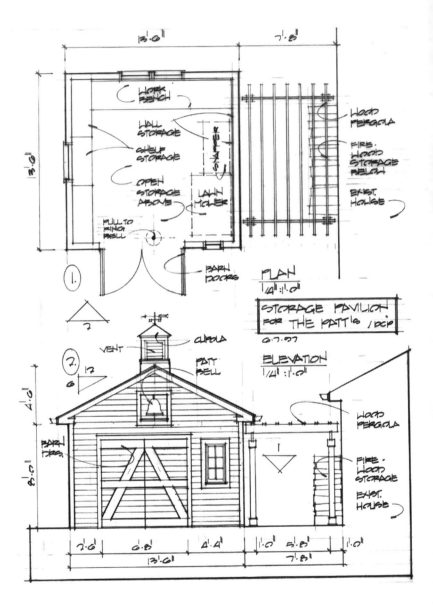

WORK BENCH
WALL STORAGE
SHELF STORAGE
OPEN STORAGE ABOVE
PULL TO RING BELL
SHAPER
LAWN MOWER
BARN DOORS

WOOD PERGOLA
FIRE- WOOD STORAGE BELOW
EXIST. HOUSE

13'-0"   7'-8"
13'-0"

1.

PLAN
1/4" : 1'-0"

STORAGE PAVILION FOR THE PATT'S / DCP
6.7.07

2.

VENT
CUPOLA
PATT BELL

ELEVATION
1/4" : 1'-0"

BARN DRS.

WOOD PERGOLA
FIRE- WOOD STORAGE
EXIST. HOUSE

4'-0"
8'-0"

7'-6"   6'-8"   4'-4"   1'-0"   5'-8"   1'-0"
13'-6"   7'-8"

A design development drawing of a storage shed. The project quickly evolved into a larger one-car garage. This hand drawing, along with sketches and discussion, was crucial in assisting the client toward expanding his program and fulfilling his needs. A simple drawing can help the owner work through ideas about space and use. This drawing shows how architects use their skills in math, language, drawing, and creativity to solve a problem and present a solution to the client. The drawing facilitated changes to the pavilion's size and shape. Even something as minor as firewood storage location was discussed and altered to avoid potential termite damage.

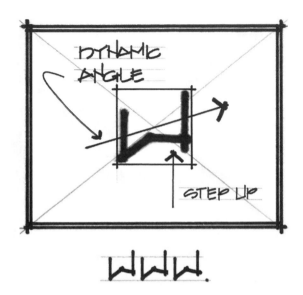

01001000 01101111 01110111
00100000 01110100 01101111
00100000 01000001 01110010
01100011 01101000 01101001
01110100 01100101 01100011
01110100 00101100 00100000
01100010 01111001 00100000
01000100 01101111 01110101
01100111 00100000 01010000
01100001 01110100 01110100
00001101 00001010

W IS FOR WWW

The Internet changed the world, and computers were the catalyst. Websites and digital machines are now universal and necessary. They are the way we communicate who we are, what we do, where we do it, and why it's done. The world has gone from typesetting to a hidden binary language of 0s and 1s. Information is conveyed on screen, disk, and file, downloadable to the world in seconds. www stands for the intangible but encompassing World Wide Web. It makes our lives easier and more complex. It embodies freedom, with relentless cycles of information at a furious pace.

Historically, architects worked with few drawings and supervised construction on site. Labor was skilled and self-directed. As demand grew for specificity, the architect's role expanded. The world grew more litigious. It also grew more complex as the variety of materials and products increased. Drawings needed more detail, and specifications become lengthy. Until recently, the architect worked with pen and ink on linen, and later on mylar and vellum. He or she reproduced drawings not

Binary code for "How to Architect, by Doug Patt." Binary code is the language of computers. It is a system for designating instructions understood by the machine. The language is a series of 0s and 1s. It is relayed in strings of a variety of lengths, called bit code. The strings correspond to a symbol or instruction.

with printers but with ammonia-based machines. Today, though design is still sometimes done with hand-drawn sketches on trace paper, most architects use computers to draw. A wide variety of software and hardware is available for this. Drawings can be created and changed at breakneck speed. Architects and engineers use computer-aided design (CAD) and building information modeling (BIM) as basic software for drawing and rendering. A wide variety of three-dimensional software is also employed to create lifelike imagery that used to take weeks or months of painstaking work.

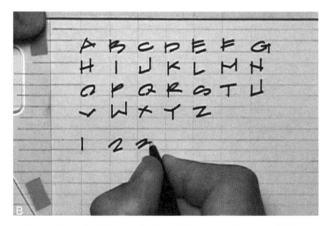

An image from the "How to Architect" Internet video called "How to write like an architect."

We do not know what the ultimate effect of the computer and the Internet on the profession will be. Websites and interconnectivity greatly streamline the management of projects. Computer software has made drawing and changes easier. Studies have shown, however, that both adults and children benefit from physically writing things rather then using a keyboard. In fact, the act of writing has been shown to engage the brain and aid in learning.[1] The same might be presumed of hand drawing and model making. As we forgo these skills in favor of automated methods, we give up something but gain elsewhere. Frank Gehry is well known for using computer software created for airplane design. His unusually shaped buildings could not have been conceived without computers and advanced software. This was once considered radical. Now many architects have adopted the practice.

1. *Wall Street Journal*, 5 October 2010, Personal Journal section.

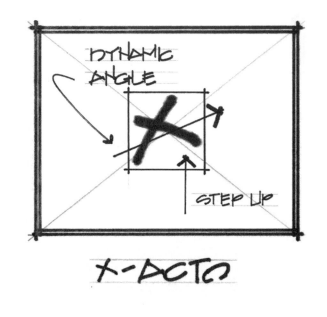

DYNAMIC ANGLE

STEP UP

X-ACTO

X IS FOR X-ACTO

X-Acto is the brand name for a cutting tool. Architects and architectural students use the X-Acto to make models and cut matboard and drawings to size. But it's clearly not their only tool. Students and professionals today use computers to draft and model; in fact, many students leave school having never used a parallel rule, triangle, or mechanical pencil. But drawing and model making by hand have not disappeared. The architect's heritage is handmade work. To some, there is nothing that can take the place of a sketch, study model, or drafted document. In case you're thinking about becoming an architect, here's a list of some hand tools that should be nearby.

A • X-Acto with small blade and larger Olfa knife, plus blades

B • 24" cutting board
   • 24" metal ruler with cork backer
   • 36" metal ruler without cork backer

C • An architect's and engineer's scale
   • Tee pins for posting drawings

D • Horsehair brush
   • Dietzgen Scum-X graphite dust remover (Scumbag)

E • Large drafting table, 36" × 60"
   • Vinyl desk cover
   • Large parallel rule, 48"
   • Architect's drafting lamp
F • 4H, 2H, HB, 2B, and 4B pencils
   • Electric pencil sharpener and eraser refills
   • 1/2" wide roll drafting tape
   • Electric eraser
   • White eraser
G • Yellow trace
   • Pentel mechanical pencil for most drafting, 5mm
   • Pens like Pentel Sign Pen, Pilot Razor Point,
     Pilot Precise Roller Ball, and Paper Mate Flair pen
   • Lettering guide for lettering work
   • Small 4" 60-degree triangle for lettering
H • Adjustable triangles, one 8" and one 12", clear
   • Metal eraser shield
   • Architect's compass
I • French curves, set of three
   • A circle template and a few ellipse templates

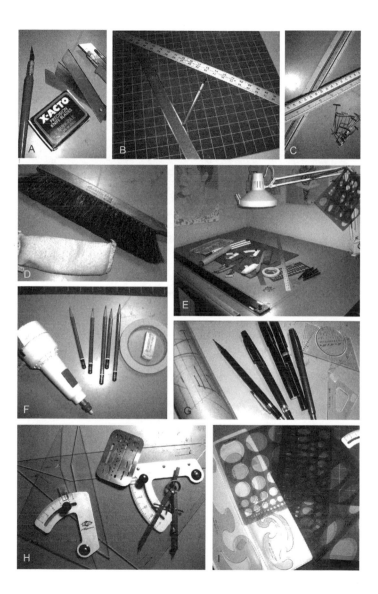

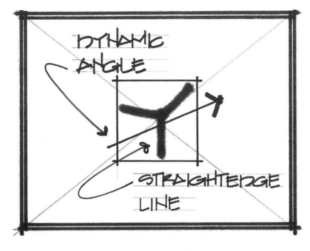

DYNAMIC
ANGLE

STRAIGHTEDGE
LINE

YOU

Y IS FOR YOU

I was once told, "Architecture is a great profession and a horrible business." No business is easy. What is great about the profession is the fact that it embodies life. It encompasses philosophy, sociology, psychology, material science, engineering, mathematics, history, construction, and creativity. Architecture is inescapable, and its history, progress, and future are an endless source of promise and enlightenment.

It's true that designing buildings, running an office, and keeping an architectural firm solvent can be overwhelming. While architectural education prepares you to be a designer, this may only be a small part of your daily work. Unless you're in a position to dictate your role in an office, your assignments may shock you. It's not unusual for an intern architect to spend months (or longer) on mundane parts of a project like window and door schedules or stair details. However, the intern architect is on a trajectory to become a project architect. The latter oversees the project after the design architect does the creative work. It's important to remember that pure design jobs are at a premium in any office, and are often reserved for tenured employees or partners. This is why some people leave one office for another, or even leave the profession forever. They can't get a job where they are allowed to design. They could go out on their own, but might not have the courage, skills, talent, contacts, or money to do so successfully. This is one of the dirty secrets of architecture. Probably fewer people would enter architecture school if they knew the truth. The great bulk of architects' work is unlike the design-centered experience taught in college.

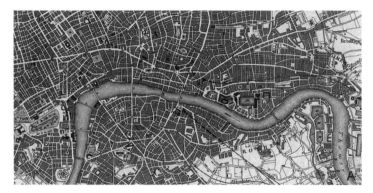

The architect's job is much like a city plan, varied and complex.

The job of an architect involves technical drawing, writing, and research. It requires understanding complex systems as well as the products, materials, and finishes that constitute a building. It also involves an extraordinary degree of coordination and organization. The architect must work with large numbers of subcontractors, contractors, consultants, and clients. The architect also needs to be able to manage the business, employees (if she's got them), and workload. In fact, these tasks can consume the work day, with no time left over for design. So understand, if you want to be an architect, that architecture is many things—not just design.

Lever House in New York City by Skidmore, Owings and Merrill, designed in the International Style and completed in 1952. Its curtain
wall construction set the precedent for the ubiquitous glass box skyscraper. SOM today has ten offices worldwide and 1,400 employees.
The size of an office affects an architect's role, opportunities, and
advancement.

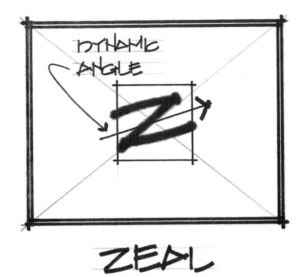

ZEAL

Z IS FOR ZEAL

Architects should not only be able to write and speak, they should continue to read long after they have graduated from architecture school. Some of my favorite books are *Experiencing Architecture* by Steen Rasmussen, *Delirious New York* by Rem Koolhaas, Frank Ching's books on architectural graphics, and Ramsey and Sleeper's *Architectural Graphic Standards*. But none of these reading experiences can equal the effect that Ayn Rand's *The Fountainhead* had on me in my youth. Generations of architects have come of age, and set their career path, because of this novel. When it was published in 1943, its publishers didn't expect much from it, but it quickly became a best seller and has remained in print ever since. It has sold something like 6.5 million copies and is still going strong.

The architect-hero architect Howard Roark epitomizes zeal. Not only does he serve as a vehicle for Rand's philosophy of objectivism, he embodies her conviction that man should be free to pursue his calling, and that individualism should triumph over collectivism. The book is based on a tension between opposing forces. Roark is passionate about modernism while his nemesis, Peter Keating, pursues conventional architecture and shallow relationships. Keating is untalented but successful. Roark is brilliant but uncompromising, his work exceptional but unappreciated. Keating is eventually destroyed by his own underhanded ways and Roark finds acceptance. In the end Keating changes a design that Roark had forbidden him to alter. There is no middle ground for Roark. He destroys the project. When he is eventually taken to court, he represents himself and makes an impassioned speech about ego, individualism, vision, and truth. He wins the case. At the end of the novel, Keating is ruined and Roark wins a skyscraper commission and, of course, the girl. Roark's impetuous pursuit of his calling is an inspiration to architects everywhere to behave with zeal, and to defend their work with principle and conviction.

Original dust jacket for *The Fountainhead* by Ayn Rand.

Postscript

Buildings are big, but the details they are made of are small. The dream of every architect is to build—not necessarily to build big, but to build what he or she imagines, without getting bogged down by obstacles along the way. The reality of practice means dealing with precisely those obstacles. So much of being an architect is about subordinating grandiose dreams to ungrandiose challenges, replacing ideal schemes with compromises. A building is full of structural and mechanical systems that must be coordinated, otherwise the building won't look or function as it should. A building must conform to local zoning ordinances. The goal of any architect is to do the work he enjoys most, yet there are many architects who even after a lifetime in the profession can never point to a building and say, "I designed that."

Architects gain experience through a variety of jobs that, in turn, make other jobs accessible. Some of these jobs will be enjoyable, others tedious. The architect works long hours and doesn't always get commensurate pay. Much of his work goes unseen. He spends late nights preparing presentations, doing design work, making changes, researching code and zoning issues, coordinating drawings, writing specifications, and working with other professionals. The finished product is often years in the making and often requires countless drawings, revisions, change orders, renegotiations, litigations, and presentations. Most of this work happens out of the sight of clients and is never seen by the public. Most of this work is necessary, much of it is unpaid.

In the United States, an architect must get a professional or master's degree, work as an intern, complete mandatory experience in specific areas of the field, and pass seven exams. Becoming a licensed architect is comparable to becoming a licensed physician in the time it takes. An architect is still considered young at forty.

The study of architecture is serious business. I received a memorable comment on my YouTube channel from an architecture student in Greece. In his first year of college, one of his professors said: "Only those who couldn't live without being architects, only those who couldn't imagine being anything different in their lives but architects, should be here." While it's a challenge to be certain of the right path, high school students might do well to test their conviction by these words.

On my first day in college, a professor told our class of more than one hundred that many of us wouldn't make it through the architecture program because of the time demands and rigors of coursework. He was right. Others, he said, would graduate but would not become architects. This was true as well. Indeed, the education of an architect (which should include a broad liberal arts sampling as well as a thorough education in the arts, architecture, and studio/design) prepares one to become a problem solver. The architect also tends to be drawn to other creative fields because of his skill set, and therefore able to consider different jobs by the time he finishes his training. It is not unusual for people trained as architects to work in product design, graphic design, model making, fashion design, furniture design, illustration, interior design, real estate development, landscape architecture, contracting, urban planning, construction management, or property management.

If you have an interest in becoming an architect, you can start testing that desire before you apply to architecture school, or even before you choose your major in college. It is never too soon to visit an architect's office, or to ask architects questions about what they do. Even in high school, you can try to obtain work in a firm as a paid or unpaid intern. Architecture has its own professional culture; working in a firm will give you a sense of that culture. Various universities also have programs that introduce students to the field. Keep in mind, however, if you decide to pursue an education in architecture, that academia and practice can be worlds apart. The transition from a theoretically or design-oriented curriculum in architecture school to the realities of practice in most firms can be jarring to say the least. Architectural education tends to focus more on the design process than on keeping the weather out, and to place more emphasis on presenting to design jurors than to zoning officials or town councils. Once employed by a firm, architects have little time to ask *why architect* the buildings they are working on. There is a client. The bills need to be paid. The architect gets to work.

Acknowledgments

Thanks to Myron Barnstone, Rudi Elert, Randy Jardee, and David Schrader for their early review of this book. A special thanks to Dr. Kevin Strauss, who made my early drafts look like an English teacher's version of redacted CIA documents. His hard work and advice added coherence and structure to a formative text. I am especially grateful to Roger Conover for choosing this book from the multitude of unsolicited manuscripts he receives, and for taking such care in reviewing the text and showing me how to improve it. Lastly, I'd like to thank the woman in the red bikini at the Florida time-share pool whom I overheard talking with an editor. Had it not been for that moment, I might never have written this book.